Praise for

"Finally a book that [bridges the gap between the] head and the heart when it comes to sales! Holly and Eric have taken a concept I have long promoted; selling is not about pushing a product or service and closing the deal, rather it is the art of mindfully discovering and then fulfilling a need and being inspired in the process. If you follow the sage advice in *Sell More, Stress Less* you will not only feel better, but your sales will soar and your soul will smile."
- J.D. Messinger, Mindful Sales 5-time award winning and #1 Amazon best seller, *11 Days in May: The Conversation that Will Change Your Life*

"*Sell More, Stress Less* is packed with 52 tips that will help even the most experienced sales professional to be more in control of their mindset and be more intentionally mindful in all their customer, prospect and team interactions. I highly recommend getting this for your sales team and working through this together to help drive more quota attainment - and keep your sales team more engaged throughout the sales process."

- Phil Gerbyshak,
VP of Sales Training, Vector Solutions

"In a world where mindfulness and sales can not only co-exist but complement each other, this is still a concept and a practice (rather than a process) that escapes most people. Holly and Eric did a great job mixing their expertise in each of these fields to create a series of steps that can be followed by both beginners and well versed sales professionals that are looking for the "it" factor that will make all the difference to their current sales results. This book introduces the reader who is open to improve their relationships and their bottom line by daring to do things differently, to a practice that can be implemented daily, in small steps that create a big impact. If you are in the business of selling a product, a service or yourself as a brand and wondering what is missing for you to become the best you can be, this book is a must read."

- Karla Merrel, The Event Maximizer,
Founder Meet & Greet Events

"Ms. Duckworth and Mr. Szymanski modeled a rarely used but powerful approach of co-presentation extraordinarily well, illustrating both how and why speakers should consider employing this technique. At the end, they transitioned seamlessly from a formal presentation into a highly informative question/answer dialog.

Attendees left enriched with readily applicable sales approaches, easily used methods for centering and focusing themselves, and, in the case of most, with Ms. Duckworth's impressive resource books. The Speakers Association of Hawaii is lucky indeed to have had this excellent presentation."

- Ethan Allen, Ph.D. Neuroscience

SELL MORE
STRESS LESS

52 TIPS

TO BECOME A
MINDFUL SALES PROFESSIONAL

**HOLLY DUCKWORTH
ERIC SZYMANSKI**

Sell More, Stress Less: 52 Tips To Become A Mindful Sales Professional

Published by Ione Publishing
Denver, CO

Copyright ©2020 Holly Duckworth, CAE, CMP, LSP. All rights reserved.

No part of this book may be reproduced in any form or by any mechanical means, including information storage and retrieval systems without permission in writing from the publisher/author, except by a reviewer who may quote passages in a review.

All images, logos, quotes, and trademarks included in this book are subject to use according to trademark and copyright laws of the United States of America.

ISBN: 978-1-7320198-3-6

Sales/ Self Help/ Mindfulness

QUANTITY PURCHASES: Schools, companies, professional groups, clubs and other organizations may qualify for special terms when ordering quantities of this title. For information, email holly@LeadershipSolutionsIntl.com.

All rights reserved by Holly Duckworth and Ione Publishing.

This book is printed in the United States of America.

IonePublishing

Contents

∽

A Note From Holly & Eric
1

Introduction
How To Use This Book
5

Part One
The Case for Mindful Sales
11

Part Two
Seven Practices To Become
A Mindful Sales Professional
17

Part Three
52 Tips to Be
A Mindful Sales Professional
45

Acknowledgments
168

Resources
170

About the Authors
171

A Note from Holly and Eric

People often ask us how we came to put sales and mindfulness together.

Out of the blue, while living across the country, Eric called Holly. Eric was achieving high sales success while, unknowingly, he was also on a collision course with anxiety and burnout which comes from unsustainable stress. Holly's business was full of mindful products and needed a boost to increase her sales efforts in order to create the lifestyle she dreamed of.

In spite of their individual successes, Holly's business needed more sales while Eric was on the verge of a serious breakdown.

Eric shared the story of his sense of overwhelm working to hit a huge, seemingly unattainable sales goal. His territory had been scaled back and his goals were increased. Eric knew he was stressed and he didn't know what to do about it. He was exercising and engaged in hobbies to offset his aggressive work schedule. After visiting his doctor and being diagnosed with ADD - Attention Deficit Disorder—Eric was prescribed amphetamines to improve his focus. The medication has side effects that include weight loss and insomnia, which created additional challenges. He did what he had always done and what he thought was the right thing to do, which was to work harder. But no matter how much harder he worked, things did not get better. As Holly listened, she began to share a few of her mindfulness techniques. Holly asked a simple question to Eric, "Did it have to be this way?" Did the process have to be stressful?" In that moment, Eric's brain took a pause. He never considered an alternative to more sales equaling more stress. Holly continued to share her mindful practices, which began to calm Eric's mind and allowed him to focus on sales with a new outlook.

At the same time, Holly was a self-employed entrepreneur who was deeply dedicated to her personal spiritual practice and mindfulness training not knowing where it would take her. It's not easy to lead a company while executing all aspects of the business, all while taking on four years of professional development courses. Holly's professional speaking, coaching and consulting business was evolving, and she was struggling to sell her ideas and topics. Holly shared stories of how she was losing business to competitors and she did not know why. Some of the competitors were more qualified and some were less qualified that she was. Some were winning the business for less money than Holly was quoting; however, some were winning for more money. It was all very confusing. As Eric listened, he began to share a few insights into the professional sales process. Eric asked a simple question to Holly, "How do you qualify your potential clients?" "Do you know there is a process to sales, and there are seven steps?" In that moment, Holly's brain took a pause. She realized that she could learn the process. No one had ever explained them to her. In the months that followed, Holly closed three new contracts that she never thought she would close by using the sales process.

We did not set out to write a book. Years ago when we became friends, we did not dream of a platform to save the lives of our friends who were suffering from stress and overwhelm. We did what we had to do to support each other through the stresses of life.

By using mindful practices, Eric is now off the ADD medications. Holly is able to write, sell and impact more people with mindful leadership and has more than doubled her sales by implementing focused, Mindful Sales processes.

Here is the truth: we are programmed to believe things are always getting upgraded, time always gets faster, and there is not enough. Here is another truth: we are not a technology device. As sales professionals, we are not robots who can always go faster or get stronger. We are human beings not human doings.

Our message is simple yet profound. We are here to tell you that the integration of mindfulness into your personal practice, as well as your work with your clients and your leadership team and co-workers is the solution. Many people don't know that there is an alternative to the stress that often accompanies sales and leadership positions. We are here to affirm that that there is another way, explain it and help you integrate it into your life.

We are open to the possibilities of asking the questions without knowing the answers. Here's to the, "I don't know," in your life, your curiosity about what mindfulness is, and your willingness to discover how, when applied to your profession, you will experience results more aligned with who you are and where you want to be. We know we have. We look forward to hearing how these practices transform your business and more importantly, your life. Please visit our website at www.LeadershipSolutionsInternational.com and use the hashtag #MindfulSales on social media and leave us your comments.

With Mindfulness and Gratitude,

Holly & Eric

Introduction:
How to Use This Book

So, what the #$%! is Mindful Sales anyway? As a mindfulness practitioner, Holly is constantly breaking things down to the smallest parts and pulling out her dictionary. Let's start there. Per the dictionary, mindfulness is "the quality or state of being conscious or aware of something." Sales is "the exchange of a commodity for money; the action of selling something."

For some, mindfulness is a lesser known word that also creates interesting energy. Some embrace it. Others are put off by the word itself.

For those who embrace the concept and fully understand the impact, mindfulness makes a difference on an individual and on those around you, your coworkers and your customers.

Mindfulness is a practice with roots in various religious and secular traditions—from Hinduism and Buddhism to yoga and, more recently, non-religious meditation. People have been practicing mindfulness for thousands of years, whether on its own or as part of a larger tradition. The word mindfulness can be traced in Pali language from the word "sati" which translates as "srti" in Sanskrit which translates to "memory" in English. In an eastern perspective, mindfulness means having the ability to hang on to current objects; remember them and not lose sight of them through distraction; wandering attention; associative thinking; explaining away or rejection. Mindfulness, once associated with Hinduism and Buddhism, among other spiritual traditions, is now becoming more mainstream. When we release any attachment to mindfulness as a religious or spiritual tradition and see it as a science, we open to the truth of the concept as both Ancient Wisdom and New Thought.

Sales is also a word that has energy for a lot of people as well. Where is your energy for sales and the selling process? For those who love sales and selling, it is a word that brings ease and joy. Then there are those for whom sales brings up the opposite energy, namely fear and frustration. Sales in the new decade will require a new integration of data with the intuitive heart we all have. With this book, we invite you to get clear about what you think about sales and create positive associations and increased sales results.

Our work together is to transform these words and concepts into a business philosophy that celebrates your high achievement with high consciousness you can attain without losing your mind.

Our intention for this book to help educate you about a new way to think, believe and act as a Mindful

Sales professional. By reading this book you will learn how to integrate mindfulness and sales to become more effective and profitable.

Mindful Sales increases your sales by:
- Reducing your stress and anxiety
- Creating focus
- Reducing overwhelm
- Increasing memory
- Improving health and happiness

Mindful Sales is a proven process that, when activated on a regular, consistent basis, helps you to take better care of you, enabling you to take better care of your customers in every stage of the sales process.

There are different ways to read this book.
- The traditional approach – read the book cover-to-cover
- The piece-by-piece approach – read one tip each week for a year
- Read it as a part of a book club or training process with your team

More important than the approach is that you put the practices we share into application in your personal and professional life. Do it now. What we know from working with adult learners is the quicker we can move a concept from etherial to application, the longer it sticks and the more effective it becomes.

Mindful Sales is not a clearly defined process nor is it a direct pathway from start to finish. In spite of this, here are seven practices to mindfully and powerfully increase your impact and your income as a Mindful Sales professional:
- Intention & Vision
- Affirmation & Beliefs
- Meet & Greet
- Qualification
- Presentation & Demonstration
- Trial Close & Close
- Follow up & Gratitude

Note these steps are not numbered. Mindful Sales is a living process that flows in this order and just like a drop of water in the river doesn't know where it's going it gets there. First learn the steps in order then customize the process for what your intuition tells you based on your unique product, service, price point and customer. At times a client may come to you with a need for a quick sale .In that case, honoring their sales process and request, you may move forward down the path to the demonstration step.

Throughout the book you will read stories of how to infuse mindfulness into your personal sales experiences. Note we work to share stories of transactions at a multitude of price points. The concept of mindfulness as a sales professional applies regardless of the price point of the product or service. Try these practices wherever you are in your sales cycle. Whether you are embarking on a new year of sales goals or if you are halfway through the year having attained only 20 percent of your goal or if you are nearly at your goal. It is commonly said in the mindful world, "There is no spot where good is not." We know the good power of applied mindfulness. If you're still skeptical, commit to five minutes a day for seven days and see how your life changes. Don't take our word for it. Try it!

This book has three parts.

In part one, we share the business case for mindfulness to help you re-frame any concerns you may have around using these applied mindfulness techniques for sales practices or introducing them to your sales team.

In part two, we break down the sales process and how to integrate mindfulness into it. This is where the greatest impact may be demonstrated while reading this book. Whether you are a seasoned professional who has been trained in traditional sales or you are new to the sales process, this section will give you valuable information to sell more with less stress for both you and your customers.

In part three, you will find 52 tips, one for each week for a year. Each tip has a story to help provide more context for you to apply Mindful Sales to your work. You will also find Mindful Sales questions to help you think about your role in the sales process in a different way. If you lead a sales team these questions can be a great starting point for shifting team culture and increasing collaboration to gain more deals. And lastly, each week we leave you with an affirmation to affirm what you want to have happen as you evolve and transform to higher levels of success as a Mindful Sales professional. Each Mindful Sales tip has with it an affirmation. An affirmation is a short, present tense statement that brings the concept of the tip to life for you. Sales is a mindset. Success is a mindset. These affirmations are shared to inspire you to live the mindful practice being presented each day.

Part One:
The Case for Mindful Sales

∞

It's natural and normal to want to resist change. Yet, we live in a world of constant change where we have to let go of what is no longer working for something that will. Our brains are hardwired for fight or flight. Most of us suffer from what many call "monkey mind." It is the sensation that there is so much to do you can't slow down and can't turn your mind off . If this is you, this book was written for you. We've been there, and like you, we choose to make a conscious effort to not to go back there.

Why does mindfulness matter in sales? Sales is a dynamic, hyper-competitive career. It's about setting and achieving deadlines often in times of adversity. In today's 24/7 global economy that is fast and speeding up, we are often required to practice being in the present moment. Many of us suffer from Mind-full ness. Our brains are so full of things to do, never allowing us to be fully present in the actual moment. As well, it is common to experience anticipatory grief or get stuck looking back and thinking about things we wish had happened or things we regret.

What is mindfulness in the sales process? Mindfulness is the practice of being present in the moment, without judgement. There are many definitions of mindfulness. Over the years this definition is starting to refine. Mindfulness is at its core awareness.

Applying Mindfulness

There are many ways to be mindful and techniques to bring you back to the present moment, to bring your brain, heart and body back to focus.

The most simple and easy way to begin a mindful practice is to become aware and observe when you are not in the present moment and then recognize your desire for awareness in the present moment. From that awakening you can move into the practice of centering your energy. Centering is the process of bringing your awareness to the present moment.

Additional suggestions include becoming aware of how you use technology. Are you managing your technology or is technology managing you? The "airplane mode" on your mobile phone works even when you are not on an airplane. Often using that function or stepping away from your phone can be a powerful tool for mindfulness.

We repeatedly address intention setting to highlight its importance. In a world that keeps us extremely busy and helps us to not feel, we must slow down to set our intentions for how we want to show up in the doing of life and work. That is intention. An example may be joyful, happy, or content.

Perhaps you are coming to mindfulness through yoga or meditation, both of which are good practices for health and wellness at work and at home. In a recent article in the Harvard Business Review, Schoostra et al. (2017) argue that mindfulness meditation works to enhance better creativity and innovation and has been observed in leading corporations like Google, Goldman Sachs and Medtronics, where they have dedicated mindfulness programs for their employees. Mindfulness practices applied through the sales process will offer the opportunity to enhance not only creativity and innovation, but also focus and clarity, all of which are required to close business. The overall impact of applied mindfulness, such as meditation to reduce stress, is increased sales to highly satisfied customers.

So, what does the practice of mindfulness look like? Mindfulness can come in lots of different forms—it could be a yoga practice that involves mindfulness, it might involve setting aside time for mindfulness meditation sessions, or it could involve practicing mindfulness during everyday activities (such as washing the dishes, as advocated by prominent Zen Master, Thich Nhat Hahn).

Thich Nhat Hanh is a global spiritual leader, poet and peace activist, revered around the world for his pioneering teachings on mindfulness, global ethics and peace.

Mindfulness can be practiced individually or as part of a group as part of a meeting or during a retreat. In fact, mindfulness is so easy you can practice it anywhere! Mindfulness can be practiced for the sole purpose of becoming more mindful and there are several mindfulness practices and organizations that are designed for specific groups of people.

One example is the Mindful Warrior Project, which helps military veterans use mindfulness to increase their well-being. There are also various groups focused on teaching mindfulness to children, such as the Kids Programme from Youth Mindfulness. The point is that no matter who you are or what your daily life consists of, there is most likely a mindfulness practice tailored to you. This versatility makes it accessible to all who are willing to learn and put in a little bit of time.

This is a key part of the philosophy of mindfulness, whether it is practiced religiously or in a secular matter. After all, mindfulness practitioners are all striving for the same thing, whether they call it mindful awareness or enlightenment. Virtually no mindfulness traditions are based on restricting their teachings to an exclusive group.

Mindfulness is a tradition with a rich history steeped in religious and, more recently, secular institutions. Anyone looking to start practicing mindfulness can choose their preferred starting point, whether it be Hindu scripture which is thousands of years old or recent Westernized teachings. This brief overview of many historical aspects of mindfulness is by no means exhaustive. It is intended to serve as a starting point to learn more about mindfulness and how to practice it. Knowing the history of mindfulness is not necessary to begin practicing it, but knowing the roots of mindfulness can help you pick the tradition and practice that will be most useful for your life and your needs. After you have found one that works for you, write us and let us know the impact it has had on your life. You might just inspire someone to start a mindfulness practice in their own life.

We all take ourselves too seriously, with a fear of failure driving the daily regiment of sales offices. Whether you are a perfectionist who will not accept anything less than an A+ on your report metrics, or you are an average sales professional who does what it takes to get by each day, we invite you to become more mindful in every part of your day.

We are not here to make extravagant promises, we are here to share with you some of the foremost thought leaders and research on the topic, simple strategies when applied daily will transform the way you think, feel and believe about mindfulness and sales.

On Holly's podcast, The Everyday Mindfulness Show, she interviewed Inna Khazan, Ph.D., author of *Biofeed-*

back & *Mindfulness In Everyday Life Practical Solutions for Improving Your Health and Performance.* Inna shares we do not need to purposefully change our physiological response to stress - we do not need to calm down - in order to do our best. All we need to do is interpret the sensations of activation in a more helpful way. Self-statements (affirmations) of "I am excited" instead of "I am anxious" or "I need to calm down" will go a long way toward helping you feel more calm, comfortable and confident and actually do better during your challenge.

In other episodes, Holly interviews Marc Lesser, author and creator of the Mindfulness programs at Google. To have instant access to these up-to-date conversations, add the podcast to your downloads by visiting www.EverydayMindfulnessShow.com.

Part Two:
Seven Practices To Be
A Mindful Sales Professional

∞

Sales people are by nature numbers people. To be a Mindful Sales professional, it is exciting to know what your numbers are, what you want them to be and to track them. Numerology is the branch of knowledge that deals with the occult significance of numbers. Have you ever found yourself seeing a set of numbers over and over? for Eric & me that combination of numbers is often 123, or 321, or 111. You get the idea. As we were preparing the various drafts of Mindful Sales, our keynote speech, all our research kept coming back to the mindful significance of seven. According to psychologists, seven fits our attention span. It is also this combination of cultural, historical, religious, numerical, and psychological factors that contribute to the allure of the number seven and the sway it has over our decisions.

According to Psychology Today, it has had significance in almost every major religion. In the Old Testament or Hebrew Scriptures, the world was created in six days and God rested on the seventh, creating the basis of the seven-day week we use to this day. In the New Testament, the number seven symbolizes the unity of the four corners of the Earth with the Holy Trinity. The number seven is also featured in the Book of Revelation (seven churches, seven angels, seven seals, seven trumpets, and seven stars). The Koran speaks of seven heavens and Muslim pilgrims walk around the Kaaba in Mecca (Islam's most sacred site) seven times. In Hinduism there are seven higher worlds and seven underworlds, and in Buddhism the newborn Buddha rises and takes seven steps. So we move forward with the Seven Practices of Mindful Sales:

- Intention & Vision
- Affirmation & Beliefs
- Meet & Greet
- Qualification
- Presentation & Demonstration
- Trial Close & Close
- Follow up & Gratitude

Let's begin with a look at each of the suggested steps.

Your choice to become a Mindful Sales professional begins before you even get to your desk, workstation or pick up the phone. It begins with careful attention to your own energy and how you want to put your energy in motion each day. That is, your sales process starts with intention.

Intention

Intention is your chief aim, how you set your energy in motion. Most of us run our lives on "autopilot," we get up each day and do what we can to survive the wave of whatever comes our way. Intention is the practice of taking each day to decide how do we want to put our energy in motion for the day. In Holly's book, Everyday Mindfulness From Chaos to Calm In A Crazy World, she teaches the power of setting a daily intention. Holly states, "whatever you focus on increases." Each day, as you practice Mindful Sales, begin with your intention before the daily task list. Select one or two positive words. Your words matter. A few sample sales intentions may be determined: excited; happy; nice; kind; balanced or love. Where you put your intention and attention you will experience growth.

Here is a mindful example. As I approached the sales process for my company in 2018 after my most successful year of keynotes, the word I chose was "allow". This intention-setting activity gave me pause to ask what does "allow" mean? Allow means "to give permission." I had to make sure I was mindfully giving myself permission to grow my company with new clients, products and services. This intention played a significant part in the growth of my company profitability by more than 20% in one year. I found it supported me in both good and interesting times. When I would get those challenging clients, I whispered to myself, "allow, allow, allow."

Vision

The best athletes in the world talk about how they visualize in their mind's eye what success for their individual sport means. For example, over the course of their career, each athlete visualizes their successful manifestation of scoring or defending, countless times. We could name the best of the best in their respective sports, Michael Jordan/Diana Taurasi, Tiger Woods/Annika Sorensam, Billie Jean King/Roger Federer, Pele/Mia Hamm, if visualization works for world class athletes, it can work for you!

Visioning as a Mindful Sales professional is the invitation to take every prospect, every sales transaction and create a vision in your mind's eye of how you want to see every step of the process to look, feel and sound. Think of your vision as your order to the Universe of how you want your sales and transactions to go. When you go to a restaurant and you place an order, you order and anticipate with 100% confidence that the food or beverage will be delivered to you in the way you ordered them. The same is true in the visioning process. The more detail you include in your Mindful Sales vision, the more likely you are to get the results you are looking for. For example, before you negotiate with a client, visualize an easy, enjoyable discussion for both you and your customer, as opposed to a difficult, tension-filled argument. Visualize both of you coming to a mutually agreeable solution where both parties are completely satisfied with the terms of the closed sale.

Do you have a vision board for attaining or exceeding your sales goals? When Holly started her company back in 2010, one of the first mindful practices she brought to life was to fill in the blanks on a contract with the ideal customer she was trying to attract. It's important to note that she did this before anyone ever requested a contract from her. She wrote in the names of her ideal clients and their respective companies, with the terms and financial compensation she expected to be agreed upon by both parties. Holly took the time (15-20 minutes) to center herself, get quiet and ask her "inner voice" who she should work with for a specific amount of money. When you calm the mind and listen, the answers appear. In that mindful quiet, Holly had the names of three companies come forward that she felt excited to work with. She also had dollar amounts that she asked to be compensated for bringing her expertise to the work. For example, she saw herself working with MNOP company, doing a consulting project for $10,000. She took that information, as strange or incomplete as it may have felt, and she opened her actual legal contract and created three mock" contracts. A short time later she found those contracts only to realize by the power of her mindfulness practice had turned into the real contracts with all three of those companies and the money circulating in her bank account.

Once you have created the vision like a movie in mind, take that vision one step closer to reality and visualize it. Place yourself into that movie. Be the one asking the right sales questions, making the powerful presentation and demonstrating your product or service in a way that inspires your prospect to purchase.

Visioning is a fun way to create what you want to have in your life. As you can see this over and over it becomes the truth in your sales funnel and book of business. Whether you cut out pictures and phrases from magazines and newspapers and put them on poster board or use an app on your computer or phone, start creating the life of your dreams by visioning and literally picturing what you want!

Affirmation

An affirmation is a positive, present tense statement of what you want to have happen. It is easy to focus on what we do not want to have happen. Come on, admit it, you've found yourself standing around the water cooler, or in the lunchroom spouting off the negative of some client interaction. Your words have power. Let's learn to share our joys and not our stresses.

When Holly works with new coaching clients one of the early homework assignments they work on is that of personalizing an affirmation for them. One client, Kari, worked on her affirmation for a few weeks to refine it. The affirmation she settled on was "I am the top salesperson at my company. I attain this award with ease and joy on December 31." Kari, at the time, was in the top

10% of her company, but needed a centering statement to keep her focus on her goals. After working with Holly and regularly repeating the statement, while feeling the joy of each sale in her, she slowly moved to win that award. What Kari learned was to believe in herself, affirm what she wanted to have happen with specific and measurable outcomes. As a result she aligned with what she wanted and made it happen, mindfully.

For every tip in this Mindful Sales training program we offer an affirmation. It is said, whatever follows the "I AM" is the I am that you are becoming.

Looking for a statement to help you remember the Mindful Sales process? Your wish has been granted.

***I AM** **Q**ualified to **P**roduce **T**houghtful **C**onditions **F**or **G**reatness*

Which corresponds to *I*ntention and *A*ffirmations *(mindfully)* *M*eet and greet *Q*ualifications *P*resentations/demonstrations *T*rial *C*lose and *F*ollow up with *G*ratitude.

Learn from Kari's example. Write a statement of what you want to have happen as a result of reading and apply the techniques in this book. If you are feeling a little uncomfortable starting, use one of the sample affirmations in section three.

Beliefs

Beliefs are strongly held thoughts that are held consciously or unconsciously to be true.

Integrating Beliefs into the Sales Process

Do you believe in yourself? Do you believe in your product or service? Are you willing and able to convey that belief in a convincing way to your customer? Do you elicit an emotional reaction within yourself when you share your product or service with someone else? If yes, is that emotion positive or negative? If you believe in yourself and you believe in your product, you will begin to feel an emotional response when you identify the ideal customer. This is where sales becomes something more than a transaction, it becomes an experience. Our invitation is for you to transcend your beliefs into an authentic, world-class customer experience.

Here is a real-life example of beliefs and how they can set you up for success. We recently encountered, Teri, a seasoned sales professional who was experiencing a drought in herr pipeline. There was no question she was in a bonafide slump. Instead of buying, new customers were not ordering and existing customers were not renewing.

Teri's confidence in converting sales was very low. Her positive mindset shifted and she did not believe she was going to sell to her customers. Before calling a customer in her pipeline, the salesperson in her already made up her mind that the customer would not buy. To compound the issue, pressure was being applied by her leaders to convert sales. As a result, when talking to customers in the pipeline, most of Teri's focus was aggressively trying to close a sale instead of being mindful and walking through the sales process with an open mind, believing the sale will close.

Prior to a sales call with a customer, we met with this professional and reminded her to meet the customer where they are and focus on building a strategic relationship with them instead of spending most of their time trying to close the sale. During the call, Teri focused her time on being mindful and fully present with the customer. The tone of the conversation was positive, supportive and engaging, which the customer appreciated. The customer shared their situation, with budget pressures and a challenging internal approval process. With her new mindful perspective, Teri shared insights and solutions that were specific to the customer's situation, leading to a follow-up call to close the business within 30 days. The shift in the belief that sales would close created more closed transactions.

Meet & Greet

The pace of life today is constructed in such a way that many of us feel compelled to stay in motion. As sales professionals, often the perception is that the faster we move, the more we will be rewarded. A Mindful Sales professional has control and understands the power of when to sit still. It is said: "Be still and know." Centering is the process of bringing your awareness back into your body.

The idea of a centered, mindful meeting with a customer sets the foundation for your sales experience. A professional greeting is simple and positive. This is an opportunity to spend time talking about anything other than your product or service. Meet the customer where they are. Did they travel a far distance to meet with you? Are they in the middle of a busy project at work? What is happening in their personal life? If you just met a person, it may be difficult to get past pleasantries; however, many times the best question to ask someone when you see them is, "How are you?"

While Eric was leading a sales team, one of his experienced managers, James, invited him to participate in a contract review meeting with a customer who was visiting from out of town. James had spoken with the customer over the phone; however, he had never met them in person. James admitted he sent the agreement without fully qualifying the business; however, he was very busy and figured he would send the agreement and work through the details and make edits once he sat down with the customer face to face.

The customer had a 2+ hour flight, and our meeting was scheduled before noon. Our office was 30 minutes from the local airport. We met the customer in the lobby of our office. After a brief exchange of pleasantries, "Hello," "Welcome," etc., we sat down and James immediately opened a paper file and started recapping the agreement. The customer appeared to be flustered and a bit overwhelmed by how quickly the conversation changed from, "hello," to "let's get down to business." The customer was an experienced professional and quickly shifted in to contract review mode.

In the moment, Eric observed an awkward back and forth between James and the customer, who were struggling to communicate their respective positions on the first page of the agreement. The energy of the meeting was off. Something was not right.

Eric interjected and asked James to please put away the agreement for a moment. He remembered that the customer was travelling. The meeting begin before noon. He put himself in the customer's shoes for a moment and asked what time they woke up to travel to the airport. "3:30 AM," the customer replied. The client also shared that they needed to wake up early because they had a long drive to their home airport. They did not get much sleep and they forgot to eat breakfast, snack or lunch before the meeting. In a moment of mindful awareness, we decided to spend the next hour talking about anything but business over lunch. The business conversation could wait.

When you invest time meeting and greeting a customer, you will learn something that will allow you to

connect in a more meaningful and substantive way.
How to integrate mindfulness into this step

Every relationship has a beginning. Choose your greeting carefully and start with something like, "Hello, my name is..." This is not the time or place for cheesy pick up lines. The best greeting is simple and establishes respect and professionalism.

As a side tip - if your sales process happens via email, be mindful of the sales meet and greet in your email. Eric & I read a lot of emails. We can tell a Mindful Sales professional from the first exchange. Use a salutation and the prospect's name in the salutation. Take the time to connect personally before selling. A sample meet and greet may look like this:

"Hello Tom, How was your weekend?"

You wouldn't meet someone on the street and say, "Tom, how was your weekend?" so give this some thought and attention as you start writing your mindful emails.

Qualification

Qualification is, without question, the most important step in the Mindful Sales process. This includes a series of questions you ask your customer before selling anything. There are many ways to do this. We focus on five key areas that can be used to better understand your customer and the reason they are looking to make a purchase.

The five key qualifying topics are:
- **N**eeds
- **D**ecision-Making Process
- **C**ompetition
- **H**istory
- **R**esources

We use the following statement to remember them.
New **D**ata **C**reates **H**appy **R**esults

Needs

Does your customer need your product or service? That's a great question in and of itself. Why do they need it? When do they need it? What will they be using it for? Who will be using or experiencing it? How will they be using it? Be sure to identify, emphasize and satisfy any need (or want) your potential customer has.

Business Needs Defined

1. A motivating force that compels action for its satisfaction. Needs range from basic survival needs (common to all human beings) satisfied by necessities, to cultural, intellectual, and social needs (varying from place to place and by age) satisfied by necessities. Needs may be finite. In contrast, wants (which spring from desires or wishes) are boundless.

Decision-Making Process

This is somewhat self-explanatory; however, it's best to break down any process through who; what; where; when; how and why. You may argue which of these takes precedence, or even priority. We recommend getting to who and when first followed by the how and why. Make sure you know who will be making the decision. Are you talking to the decision-maker? It's common for a non-decision maker to gather information for a decision maker. The decision maker could be a single person or a group of individuals. Be sure to ask as many questions as you can when it comes to decision making. If you know how the buying decision is being made, you can direct your efforts to align with the mindful outcome of directing your customer to the best solution/outcome for their situation.

Competition

Is your product or service unique and what is your Unique Selling Proposition (USP)? Chances are you have at least one competitor. Make sure you ask your potential customer if they are considering options. The most basic of any business curriculum teaches a professional to get more than one bid before purchasing a product or service. Think about it. Do you buy the first thing you see without looking at other options? Look around you right now. Every product or service you see will more than likely have an alternative that costs the same, more or less. Competition is a good thing and the consumer usually benefits from it. Competition is healthy in business. Don't be afraid of and make sure you do not skip this question.

History

Has your potential customer (ever, recently) purchased your product or service before, either from you or from one of your competitors? If they have, ask what they liked about it and what they did not like about it. If they have not, that's ok; however, be sure to ask as many questions as possible, within reason, to seek understanding as to what their expected outcome of the purchase is. Set realistic expectations about what can go right and also what may not go right based on both of your past experiences.

Resources

For the purpose of sales, the term resources refers to "currency or other assets that may be exchanged for goods or services." Financial resources may be assumed with smaller purchases, as they are typically exchanged at the time of purchase. If you want to buy consumer goods in person or on-line, you typically have to present payment before receiving the product. For larger purchases, it's perfectly acceptable to ask, "how are you going to pay for this?" In addition, if credit is requested, it's fully expected that you will ask many questions to minimize risk and get paid for your work.

How to integrate mindfulness into this step

Let's continue the sales conversation with the out of town customer who flew in to meet with Eric and his sales manager, James. After meeting and greeting the client, it was important to spend time further qualifying the business before moving in to the specific contract discussion. We filled in the missing gaps by asking questions in the qualifying topics above. We invited the customer to ask questions along the way. Once we finished fully qualifying the business, we had the answers to the questions needed to complete the contract agreement.

Qualification should be a conversation, not an interrogation. Recognize that if you do not have rapport with your customer, they may not be willing to share all of their details with you. Trust, credibility and relationships are built over time.

If your customer resists giving you details, do not display anger or frustration. Be patient, humble and kind throughout any fact-finding exercise. For small purchases, the answers may come quick and easy. For larger purchases and complex sales, it may take more than one conversation to see the full picture. Forgive yourself if you perceive this as not going well at any time during the sales process. There is a saying that, "If you want to build a skyscraper, you need to pour a deep foundation." Once again, building relationships takes time.

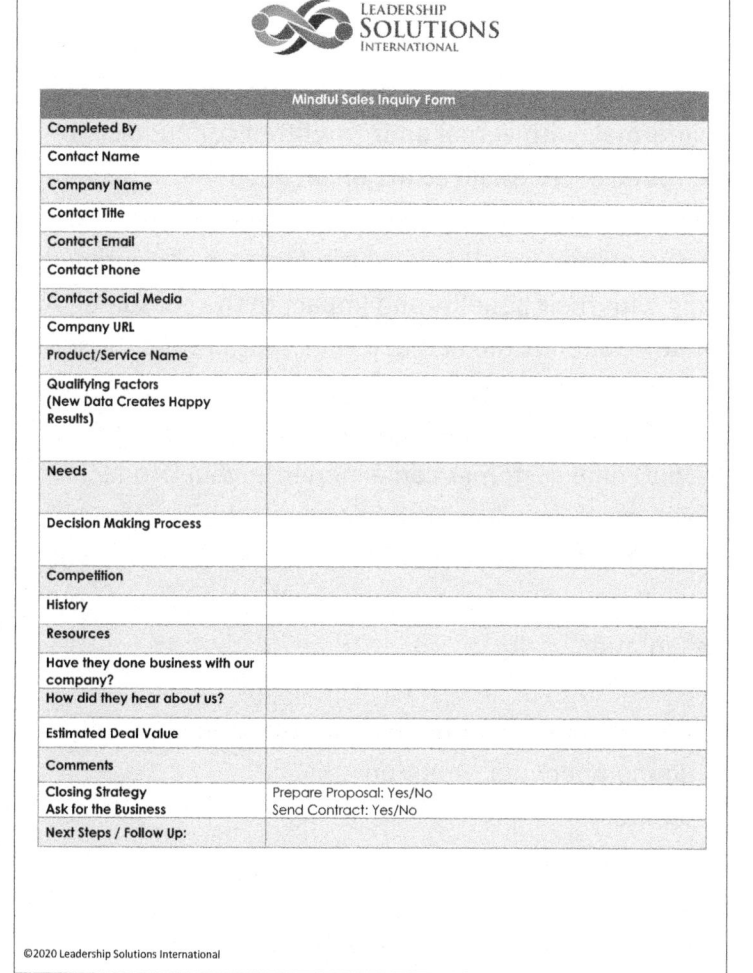

	Mindful Sales Inquiry Form
Completed By	
Contact Name	
Company Name	
Contact Title	
Contact Email	
Contact Phone	
Contact Social Media	
Company URL	
Product/Service Name	
Qualifying Factors (New Data Creates Happy Results)	
Needs	
Decision Making Process	
Competition	
History	
Resources	
Have they done business with our company?	
How did they hear about us?	
Estimated Deal Value	
Comments	
Closing Strategy Ask for the Business	Prepare Proposal: Yes/No Send Contract: Yes/No
Next Steps / Follow Up:	

©2020 Leadership Solutions International

Figure 1. Mindful Sales Inquiry Form

Presentation/Demonstration

A presentation gives information to the client about your product or service. Presentations may be formal or informal, with verbal and/or written communication such as an overview given in person or on-line. A presentation of your product shows the correct way to use the product or service. This is where features are outlined along with their benefits and impact to the consumer. A demonstration is the actual use of your product or service. Think of a free sample in a food court or a test drive of a vehicle. This is usually a key moment of truth where the potential customer can experience your product or service for themselves. This is perhaps the most important part of the sale, where the customer can see if you can deliver on the promises you made throughout your presentation.

How to integrate mindfulness into this step
  Remember your Intention
  Center
  Breathe
  Keep your beliefs positive
  Focus on your positive vision

Make sure you answer the question, "What's in it for me," which is always present in the client's mind. Be fully present at the time of the presentation and demonstration, with a focus on accuracy. Continue to create the vision here. So many people want to jump ahead and attempt to close the business before providing a thoughtful and thorough presentation and demonstration. Resist the urge to skip this important step. Allow yourself and your prospect to honor the process of mutual learning and discovery which takes place. Recently, while shopping for a home, we encountered a listing for a property on a leading real estate website/search engine. The company which operated the search engine also owned the property. On the website, there were many details listed about the property, including number of bedrooms and bathrooms, square footage, general area information and specific items that were included with the home, including appliances. The home was in an area we liked and it was in the target price range that we included in our spending plan. We contacted our realtor and scheduled a tour of the home. In this case, the presentation of the property was a self-guided tour of the listing on the real estate search engine. The demonstration was the tour of the home which was provided by our real estate agent.

Trial Close & Close

A trial close is a fact-finding question, or series or questions, used to determine the customer's level of interest in buying your product or service. This is typically used strategically before closing the sale as a way to show if the customer is ready to buy. Do not be discouraged if the customer is not ready to buy when you are ready to sell. A Mindful Sales professional is patient and is understanding that decision-making on a purchase is not always aligned with a month-end sales quota.

Closing the sale is plainly and simply asking for the business, confirming the sale or the achievement of a "desired outcome." It is the ultimate moment of truth. Are we doing this or not? Closing comes in many forms and it may bring anxiety to the sales professional. Human nature may involve a certain fear of rejection. Who wants to be told no, or they are not being selected? If you have engaged with all of the steps of the Mindful Sales process, and your potential customer is aligned with your product or service, closing should be a natural and stress-free part of the process. Whether or not you are selected is something you can learn from. Keep your dignity throughout both winning or not winning the business, and this will be rewarded in future (think referrals, etc.).

If you consider the previous example of purchasing a home, our realtor asked trial close questions as we walked through each room. "How do you like the kitchen?" "Do you see yourself entertaining in the backyard?" "These cabinets are dated; however, you could easily paint them or maybe change them out. Does that sound like something you would be interested in doing?" After completing the walk through, she attempted to close the sale by stating, "It sounds like you really liked the location, the general condition and the overall layout of this home," and then she asked, "Would you like to make an offer on this home?" The answer was easy. "Yes," we replied. If we could get the home at the price we were willing to pay, we were ready to complete the purchase. After two rounds of negotiation with the seller, we arrived at a mutually agreeable price, and we purchased the property.

How to integrate mindfulness into this step

The trial close/close step is commonly believed to be the hardest step of the sales process. Therefore it is a huge opportunity for you to infuse mindful practices. In Holly's book, Mindful Leadership The A to Z Guide for Stress-Free Leadership, she provides a mindful leadership practice and coloring mandala for every step of the Mindful Sales process. The corresponding mandalas for the "T" in Trial the "C" in Close are Trust and Center, respectively. As you grow your mindfulness practice, trust and continuously refer to the seven steps and you will be guided on what to do, what not to do and how to move to the highest and best outcome of every sales exchange.

Remember your intention
Center
Breathe
Keep your beliefs positive
Focus on your positive vision

Additional mindfulness notes for trial close

Create a list of some trial closes to practice with by yourself, before meeting with your customer(s):

Is this working?

Are we making progress?

Am I being mindful in this moment?

Am I fully present with the customer demonstrating connection to them authentically?

Are we moving closer to a solution/sale or are we moving farther away?

Reaffirm - Restate Your Affirmation

Reaffirm if the customer is responding in a positive way. If they are responding positively, meet them with the same positive energy they are sharing with you. If they are not responding positively, don't fall into their negative energy. Return to your centered, calm energy, affirming what you want to have happen.

Follow Up & Gratitude

The sales cycle is never ending. It evolves, flows and repeats itself the next time a customer is looking to make a purchase. Congratulations if you won the sale. Celebrate the victory and begin the follow up of delivering on the product or service that was sold. If you sold any product or service, follow up would include making sure the product works or service is delivered as agreed with the customer in the previous steps in the sales process. Remember to express thanks, gratitude and/or appreciation in an appropriate way.

On the flip side, if you did not win the sale, follow up may include asking for feedback as to why you lost the business, learning from the situation and using the information to help win business in the future. Regardless of whether you are given feedback, this is also a time to express thanks, gratitude and/or appreciation for their time and consideration. Yes, you still thank the customer when you do not win the business. That is what sets apart a Mindful Sales professional from any other salesperson. In the spirit of, "if at first you don't succeed, try, try again," keep your head up and invite the client to consider you in the future. You never know, they may have chosen a product or service that does not work. You just might get the business after all. The odds may be low of this happening; however, it does happen, so keep your integrity and professionalism in the highest and best at all times.

After agreeing to purchase the home, we went back and reviewed the listing on the real estate website several times. We noticed something interesting that did not come up in the purchase agreement. The website advertised two major appliances would be included in the purchase; however, they were not included in the countersigned agreement. This was a reminder for both the buyer and seller to pay attention to the details throughout the transaction. Long story short, the appliances were not included in the purchase agreement, so there was no legal obligation for the seller to include them in the sale. We asked our realtor to clarify the seller's intention as to the reason the items would be advertised on their website and not included in the purchase agreement. This was a fair question to ask, even though we had a signed agreement. After all, the seller was a publicly traded corporation who actually owned the website with the incorrect information. The person at the company who created the listing may have just been going through the motions in a mind-less way. Small mistakes like checking the wrong box in their software could have cost them a sale or perhaps could have negated some of the profit from the transaction.

How to integrate mindfulness into this step

Integrating mindfulness in the follow up and gratitude is taking a moment to feel gratitude in your body as the truth of your experience. Don't just say you are grateful, feel it! Feel joy in your body. Share that joy with your potential customer/lead/prospect.

Remember your intention
Center
Breathe
Keep your beliefs positive
Focus on your positive vision

Mindful Sales is a joy-filled, easy process when you set that intention early, often and throughout the sales process. When Eric came to Holly stressed and overwhelmed and she asked him, "does it have to be this way?" she changed the way he thought about his interaction with customers before, during and after the sale. When you look at the steps before, intention setting, centering and give yourself the awareness, mindfulness of what you want to have happen in the most positive way, you begin to attract to you positive sales experiences.

As you move to the meet and greet, qualification, presentation and demonstration phases taking the practices of positive beliefs, powerful vision and affirmation with you not only make selling more fun but more profitable. As you move through the seven steps concluding with trial close, close and gratitude, you activate the power of mindfulness. Do these steps, with awareness and mindfulness, and you will achieve world-class results.

As a Mindful Sales professional, it's key to remember that gratitude is also conveyed as a thank you gift of some sort. If you have the opportunity to provide a gift, don't miss this opportunity to reconnect with your customer. Is there something you learned in the meet and greet process that may inform a personal gift? One of Holly's favorite examples of this dates clear back to 2003. She was planning an event at an outdoor garden venue. The event had multiple vendors from rental of chairs, audio-visual and catering. At the end of the event, the manager of the catering company asked to meet Holly. Over tea the salesperson presented her with a red chinese food box, inside was a royal blue and white orchid flower with a lovely handwritten note. This gift was a direct reflection of the relationship the salesperson had built with Holly as the venue was the Portland Classical Chinese Garden and her favorite color was blue. Still today, Holly has the gift on her desk and remembers this thoughtful, Mindful Salesperson.

Every story has a beginning, middle and end. The same is true with every sales situation you encounter. Now that you have seen the Mindful Sales process, including the practices to become successful, we recommend that you keep this book close to your office or work location as a reference. If you're stuck in a sales situation that is not moving forward, be sure to identify where you and your customer are in the sales process and apply the mindful practices shared in the preceding paragraphs. When in doubt, go back to the beginning - Meet & Greet, followed by Qualification. If you need to repeat the presentation and/or demonstration, repeat the presentation and/or demonstration. Believe in yourself and believe in your product. Ask questions along the way to reaffirm understanding and, of course, ask for the business. After you win or lose the sale, be sure to follow up and express gratitude along the way. Talk through challenging situations with a team member or coworker. Invite them to read this book so you can collaborate with a common objective of selling more with less stress.

Share Your Stories
∾

We can't wait for you to share your stories with us
and the online Mindful Sales community
by using hashtag #MindfulSales
on your favorite social network.

Part Three:
52 Tips To Mindful Selling

∞

Over the past several years we have learned that Mindful Sales takes practice. It is not always perfect. It is the practices you repeat that increase your perfection. Now you are ready to move these practices off the page and into your life. Integrating mindful stress reduction and focus strategies into your success as a sales professional takes time. Time that you may be telling yourself you simply do not have. In order to help you re-program this belief, we offer a guide with tips that provide areas of focus for you and your sales team (if applicable). Here we provide for you one simple mindful practice integrated into what you are already doing as a sales professional to practice mindfulness each week of the year. NO need to wait till January 1 to begin. You can start this practice anytime.

Read the tip, explore the Mindful Sales concept with the Mindful Sales thought-provoking question. Then use the weekly affirmation to keep your head and heart focused on providing the customer a solution and a sale that is mutually beneficial for all.

SELL MORE, STRESS LESS

Talk can sometimes be cheap and words can be limiting. We wrote this book to share the Mindful Sales philosophies and to help you put them into action. We can tell you, with conviction, that you will get results by selling in the moment. You now have the knowledge, it's time to sell more with less stress. Here are the fifty-two tips to help you become a Mindful Sales professional.

"Reading about mindfulness and not completing the exercises is like going to a restaurant and reading the menu without eating." John Kabat-Zinn

We invite you to share your success stories on social media by using the hashtag #MindfulSales.

1

All Things Begin and End With Intention

~~

Great sales start before the sale. In fact, long before the sale. Mindful Sales begin when you set your intention to be a high-valued sales professional.

An intention is how you choose to put your energy in motion in the sales process. Will you choose to be kind in your selling or will you choose to be forceful? We have all come across both types of sales professionals, those who offer or invite you to try the product and those who demand. There is no one way to sell or one exact formula. There is what works for you. Will you set an intention for curiosity, calm, stress or success? Choose your energy carefully to see the mindful results you seek.

The intention of abundant, easy sales often results in abundant signed contracts or sales.

Mindful Sales Question for Consideration

What is my intention for selling this week, month or year?

_____

_____

_____

_____

_____

Affirmation

∽

I am clear in my intention to improve the ease and joy in my sales process.

2

Be Present Fully During the Entire Sales Experience

~~~

Any successful sales process takes time. Every product or service has its own sales lifecycle. The common belief is that smaller dollar sales may be quick and maybe even easy to sell. As the size of a transaction increases, the amount of time to complete the sales process typically increases. Note that it is a belief. This may not always be the case; when in doubt, be present and guide your thoughts, feelings and actions accordingly.

Mindful Sales Question for Consideration

How will I be fully present with my sales leads, prospects and clients this week to let go of mindless distractions and be fully with them and the sales process?

_____

_____

_____

_____

_____

Affirmation

∞

I am fully present in my body,
mind and spirit as I move the sales process
forward in more positive ways for
myself and my clients.

3

Price is a State of Mind

〜

As a Mindful Sales practitioner you must quickly learn that what you think about you bring about. So what you think of your price point and products becomes a direct reflection of your success in the sales cycle.

A common question most sales professionals encounter is, "How much does it cost?" A Mindful Sales professional ensures that the focus of the conversation is not just about price. One of the first professional sales courses taken by Eric early in his career was written by Joe Verde. Joe advises to "stay off price" as often as possible. Yes, everyone wants to talk about price at some point. Just make sure it's not the only thing you are talking about. There is so much more to discuss that will lead to a successful sales encounter.

Mindful Sales Question for Consideration

How can I increase my comfort talking about the features, benefits and the price of the products that I sell?

_____

_____

_____

_____

_____

Affirmation

∞

I know my product is priced at the right price point for my ideal target customer and the value I deliver.

4

Walk The Path and Trust the Process

When you bake or cook, it's usually best to follow a recipe. Think of the seven steps of professional selling as a recipe for success that has been proven over time. If you were to put all of the ingredients in a bowl, mix them together and casually toss them in the oven for a random amount of time, chances are the outcome will not be what you desire. However, if you follow the recipe, using the ingredients specified in the order that was recommended, at the correct temperature for the suggested amount of time, the results will be what you expect. Of course, at home chefs may tweak the recipe to give it a personal touch or signature. The same applies to professional sales. The overall process is tried and true; however, you may find ways that vary slightly to maximize your individual style or situation.

Mindful Sales Question for Consideration

How can I trust my own intuition more to improve my sales process and close rate?

_____

_____

_____

_____

_____

> Affirmation
>
> ∞
>
> I allow my intuition to guide the sales process knowing the questions I ask, the answers I receive and the product/service I sell is guided by Spirit.

5

Sacred No & Sacred Yes

It is important to remain professional at all times, especially when you do not close a sale. The actions you take when you lose a sale may have a direct impact on your future sales. After working with a repeat customer for nearly a year, we scheduled a meeting to finalize the details of the contract. We arrived at the meeting and were notified that a change in decision came from leadership, and we didn't get the business. Without skipping a beat, in the moment, we smiled, genuinely thanked the customer for the opportunity, and asked if we could revisit this at another time. In that moment, the customer said to us, "Yes, and your response in this moment is the reason we will always do business with you in the future." They went on to elaborate that in the past, they had a similar experience with one of our competitors. Upon notifying the sales professional they were not selected, they became upset and negative about their disappointment. The customer was made to feel like they did something wrong. It is important to not let your disappointment show in a negative way. While it's great to win, try to make losing the best experience possible. Learn from it and move forward to the next opportunity.

Mindful Sales Question for Consideration

What have I learned from my past two leads who said "no" that will allow me to get one step closer to my next "yes?"

_____

_____

_____

_____

_____

> Affirmation
>
> ∞
>
> I recognize that every "no" is one step closer to the right "yes" for my product/service offering.

6

Trust is a Two-way Street

∞

Building trust is a two-way street during the sales process. A Mindful Sales professional should always seek to earn their customer's trust. A customer may or may not realize that they also have a responsibility to demonstrate that they can be trusted to fulfill their obligation of a sale.

Mindful Sales Question for Consideration

Where am I doubting myself as a Mindful Sales professional? How can I build trust in me to build trust in the sales process and close more deals?

_____

_____

_____

_____

_____

> ### Affirmation
>
> I am the right salesperson at the right time with the right and perfect clients.

7

Trust Time

∞

Every customer with a desire always has a timeline of when they want that desire to be met. Time is an interesting human concept that we all agree upon. When I say we are having lunch at noon you know when that is. This is not the case with the sales process as everyone has their own sense of time. For example, someone may want to buy a travel trailer. Seems easy, right? Well maybe we need to use our own sense of the Mindful Sales process to learn more. Do they want to buy that travel trailer at the beginning of the outdoor season to travel or wait until the end of the year to get the best deal? Be careful to pay attention to what you believe about time and what your customer wants.

Mindful Sales Question for Consideration

How can I step back as a Mindful Sales professional and give my clients the time they need to build value and invest in the product or service I am selling?

_____

_____

_____

_____

_____

> ### Affirmation
>
> ∞
>
> I recognize that time is a human construct and that there is only the divine alignment of client wants and my abilities to fulfill them.

8

Welcome Home

∞

A question you can ask yourself is, "Are you a good host?"

When you welcome someone into your home you do not simply let them walk in. You greet them. As a Mindful Sales professional you should welcome someone into your sales center in person or over a conference call or virtual environment the same way.

Mindful Sales Question for Consideration

Am I welcoming prospects into my sales process with the same ease and joy as welcoming friends into my home? How can I adjust this process to increase my Mindful Sales?

_____

_____

_____

_____

_____

> ### Affirmation
>
> ∾
>
> I am balancing my head energy and my heart (passion) energy to allow my product to be purchased by the right person at the right time for the right and perfect reason.

9

Let Me Hear My Body Talk

∞

If you're happy and you know it, tell your face! Have you ever visited a performing group, like a choir or musical group? Does the facial expression of the individual(s) singing a happy song match the words in the song? If you concentrate fully in the moment, you may find your facial expression will not always match your intention during the sales process. This is something you can practice in front of a mirror or by using the selfie-camera on your smart device. Simply being aware of this is a step in the right direction. Be sure to practice a welcoming, mindful body language throughout the sales process.

Mindful Sales Question for Consideration

Is my body language open and inviting or am I closed? How can I be more aware and mindful about how my body language is making prospects want to buy from me?

_____

_____

_____

_____

_____

> Affirmation
>
> ∞
>
> I am comfortable in my body as a Mindful Sales professional. I look good, I feel good and I am good at sales.

10

Voice & Value

～

Every sales conversation takes a natural tone of voice. Are you mindfully aware of the tone you set and how you meter your tone to that of your customer and the situation? One client we were coaching sold shoes in a very busy shoe shop. Maybe you know the one with the loud rap music and the high energy feel. In order to have success in that scenario, the salesperson had to speak up, talk loud and listen carefully. His tone of voice had to be high energy to connect to the customer and the loud, colorful shoes he was selling. On the opposite side of the sales spectrum, we have worked with sales professionals in the high-end jewelry business, with the quiet soft music and the intimate little spaces for conversation. A sales professional in that environment must share a different conversation.

Mindful Sales Question for Consideration

How does my tone and volume of my voice effectively articulate and connect me to my prospect?

_____

_____

_____

_____

_____

Affirmation

I use my voice in powerful ways to share my excitement for the product/service I sell. I know my voice is loud when it needs to be loud, quiet when it needs to be soft and always shared in kind service to my prospect.

11

Start with a Question

People don't know how much you care until you show them that you care.

Hello, my name is {insert name here}, how are you today? Notice this is not always, "how may I help/assist you." One slight shift in genuinely asking about the person instead of starting with an offer to assist allows you to be present in the moment with your customer. Do this during every encounter and anticipate that the response may be positive if they are having a good day, neutral or even negative if they are not having a good day. As you offer your name, ask the name of your sales prospect. Demonstrate your mindful listening by using their name during the steps of Mindful Sales. Remember that customers are people, too. Meeting them where they are energetically is an excellent practice for the Mindful Sales professional.

Mindful Sales Question for Consideration

What question is authentic to me to demonstrate a genuine connection between me and my interest in the customer before, during and after the sale?

_____

_____

_____

_____

_____

> Affirmation
>
> ∽
>
> I use mindful curiosity and discovery to demonstrate I care for the prospect and the sales process beyond the initial sale.

12

The Choice is Yours

~

It may surprise you to learn that most customers have been mistreated during a sales encounter over their lifetime. While it may not be fair, they may bring these negative experiences to your sales experience with them. It's ok to say something like, "it sounds like you have had a bad experience in the past. I'm really sorry to hear that and I want to earn your business the right way (or similar)."

Mindful Sales Question for Consideration

What is my belief about sales as a profession? How does this belief contribute to my current level of sales success?

_____

_____

_____

_____

_____

Affirmation

I am a Mindful Sales professional delivering a positive sales experience for all prospects, leads and clients regardless of sales outcomes. I am aware that my presence is a present to those with whom I work at every level.

13

Power of the Pause Button

When you first encounter a customer, resist the urge to begin selling your product or service until you have had a chance to meet them and find common ground through meet and greet and qualification. This can be difficult in the world of overwhelm and limited time. Trust in this discipline and your customer will appreciate the courtesy and respect you show to them.

Mindful Sales Question for Consideration

What are three questions I can ask a lead or prospect in the introductory steps of mindful selling to demonstrate genuine care and concern and build authentic rapport? Today I intentionally create two-three minutes of mindful non-sales conversation with each lead or prospect I meet. I do this from the absolute knowing that no matter the sale, I show each person care and awareness.

_____

_____

_____

_____

_____

Affirmation

I believe in the power of the Mindful Sales process to transform my sales process with ease, fun and joy.

14

Quiet Your Quota

∞

Sales quotas can be daunting. The stress of achieving a certain number of client calls should create a sense of urgency in your day. Remember to respect a customer's time; however, being mindful during the sales process allows you to be present with your client and focus on their needs so you can provide the right solution to them.

Mindful Sales Question for Consideration

What does it look like, feel like and sound like to meet my monthly/quarterly or annual quota? Take five minutes this week to feel into the absolute knowing that your quotas are met or exceeded.

_____

_____

_____

_____

_____

Affirmation

∞

I affirm and know that I meet my sales quota in fun and powerful ways.

15

Be Still and Know. Start at the Beginning

∞

As a Mindful Sales professional you will need to practice listening more than you talk in order to gain knowledge and rapport with your prospect.

It has been said that the journey of 1,000 miles begins with one step. In the world of overwhelm and chaos, you may feel the urge to go straight to the Closing step. Take a deep breath and start at the beginning of the Sales Process - Meet & Greet. Be present in the moment with your customer. If you are feeling stressed, pause for a moment, breathe in and out, and smile. Welcome your customer and thank them for taking the time to meet with you.

Mindful Sales Question for Consideration

What is my intention? How will I start this sales conversation with mindful, positive intention and maintain that through all of the steps?

_____

_____

_____

_____

_____

Affirmation

∞

I am thankful and grateful for the opportunity to explore an opportunity with this person. I trust the sales process.

16

Prioritize Human Being vs Human Doing

～

It is important to take your sales profession seriously; however, every now and then try to remember that most sales experiences are not a life or death situation. Take it seriously, just be aware not to over do it as you forget about the big picture. Commerce is an important part of a healthy society.

Mindful Sales Question for Consideration

How can I be a human being today?

_____

_____

_____

_____

_____

> ### Affirmation
>
> ∞
>
> I am a human being, I choose how I will "be" today. I will be kind as I offer my product/service to people who can benefit from my offering.

17

Be Without Judgment

∽

Avoid stereotypes at all costs. The cliche that works best here is "Don't judge a book by its cover." You don't always know if a client will buy based on their appearance. You may recall that in the movie, *Pretty Woman*, the scene where Julia Roberts walked in to an expensive store and a sales person passed up the opportunity to work with them. The sales professional who stepped up and welcomed her with open arms sold to most of them. This was a commission-based job. Remember, it's not the job of a sales professional to determine whether a customer is qualified before fully completing the qualifying step.

Mindful Sales Question for Consideration

How can I release judgment to increase my sales close rate?

_____

_____

_____

_____

_____

> **Affirmation**
>
> ∞
>
> I see each person who comes into my company in a positive light with highest intention knowing we can make the right sales fit.

18

The Budget is Always Wrong

During the qualification stage, one of the important questions is about resources. In other words, does the customer have the ability to pay for the goods or services. A Mindful Sales professional is prepared to ask more than, "Can you afford it?" Think, "How can you afford it?" Even if the customer does not have the money, they may have additional resources, like a sponsor or individual who will be buying this on their behalf. Asking a potential customer, "What is your Budget for this?" sometimes exposes them for not knowing the answer. It's an honest response, even if they walk in "knowing" the answer. This may change during the sales process as they learn more about your product or service. The budget may go up or down, depending on how the encounter goes. If you have a large variance in pricing between your products (entry level to high-end luxury, for example), you may find the a customer thinks their budget is in the luxury category when their known resources are in the entry level category. Be mindful of keeping your customer's dignity in tact as you shift your sales presentation towards the entry level EVEN IF YOU WILL MAKE LESS MONEY FROM THEM. Treat everyone with dignity and respect, and you will be rewarded with increased sales.

Mindful Sales Question for Consideration

How can I listen a little closer to get better information from my lead or prospect on their budget requirements?

_____

_____

_____

_____

_____

> **Affirmation**
>
> ∞
>
> I am open to make more revenue and decrease the expense, resulting in better financial returns.

19

Believe in Good Competition

~~

There is a reason for competition it motivates us and makes us better. The primary beneficiary of competition in the marketplace is usually the customer. Be grateful for your competition. Learn about their product or service, and also learn about your counterpart in their organization. Treat them with respect and your results will improve.

Mindful Sales Question for Consideration

Do I know who all of my competitors are? Do I fully understand my competition? Am I willing to bless them knowing that the good I give in the world will come back to my sales transactions?

___

___

___

___

___

Affirmation

∞

I celebrate the success of my competitors, knowing there is only collective good. When good goes to my competition, it is on it's way to me also.

20

Past is not Bound by Precedence

Wisdom keepers (we don't say old people) will tell you how important it is to learn from the past. Your customer has a history of purchasing. Make time to learn about whether this is their first time making a purchase of this type of product, or if this is their 100th time. Even if they have made the purchase before, ask about their experience. Was it positive or negative? Recognize and acknowledge the outcome of their history and ask how they would like this experience to unfold.

Mindful Sales Question for Consideration

How have I developed as a Mindful Sales person with each selling transaction I have handled?

_____

_____

_____

_____

_____

> **Affirmation**
>
> ∞
>
> I honor that people and their needs change.
> I am with my clients and their needs
> fully now.

21

What You Believe, You Bring About

If you are preparing for a test, do you study or just "wing it?" It is typically easier to take a test if you have taken the time to prepare, study and learn about the material on the test. This is the same process decision makers go through before making a purchase. Choose to guide a customer and become a study partner in their learning group.

Mindful Sales Question for Consideration

What do I believe about my ability to close the sales with the clients with whom I am currently working?

_____

_____

_____

_____

_____

Affirmation

My close rate is increasing and my income and impact in the world is expanding.

22

Begin Again –
Do You Really Know Them, Now?

∞

"The only true wisdom is in
knowing you know nothing."
- Socrates

If you think you know a repeat customer, be mindful to not fall in to the trap of assumption. Your customer has never been the person they are at this time in their life. While their past experiences may be an indicator of future behavior, it is not a guarantee. Things change. Circumstances change. Resources change. The only constant is change.

Mindful Sales Question for Consideration

How are you different as a sales professional than when you first started your career? Is it possible your clients have changed as well?

_____

_____

_____

_____

_____

Affirmation

∞

I allow myself to be new in the sales process and my clients to be new also, resulting in new sales and service opportunities for all of us.

23

Selling With All Five of Your Senses is the Most Mindful Gift you can Give to Yourself and Your Customers

∽

Gently begin presenting your product after you have spent time getting to know your customer, how they are feeling in the moment and after they have shared their qualifying information. See if you can engage as many of your customers' five senses as possible (if applicable) during your presentation, including sight, smell, hearing, taste and touch. The purpose of engaging the senses is to invoke a positive feeling or emotion throughout the sales process.

Mindful Sales Question for Consideration

What is the strongest of my senses? What is the weakest of my body senses? How can I use my strongest sense as a sales advantage? How can I use my weakest as a sales opportunity for growth?

_____

_____

_____

_____

_____

> Affirmation
>
> ∞
>
> As a Mindful Sales professional I use my hearing, smelling, tasting, seeing, and feeling to maximize every sales opportunity.

24

Move Forward with Mutually Agreeable Next Steps

～

As a Mindful Sales professional, it's best if you and your client make decisions together. If one party is ready to move forward and the other part is not, there is a lack of agreement. For example, if a customer wants to move forward at 50% of the price you are willing to sell, it is not possible to move forward. If you are selling a product for more than the customer is willing to pay, it is not possible to move forward. This tip does not just apply to price, it applies to every part of the sales process..

Mindful Sales Question for Consideration

Where am I in the sales process with each one of my customers? Do we have mutually agreeable next steps? If not, go back and gain that powerful agreement.

_____

_____

_____

_____

_____

Affirmation

∞

I trust my intuition and ask my clients for mutually agreeable next steps as we move forward to close each and every sale.

25

Patience is a Virtue. Close with Care.

Patience is a virtue. How many times have you skipped to the last pages of a book without reading the entire story? If you go back and read the story, you will likely find that there were a lot of details you missed that contributed to the outcome. Be patient and resist the urge to skip to closing. Remember, your sales presentation is the Wednesday of your work week. You're about halfway there.

Mindful Sales Question for Consideration

How can I increase my sales rate by waiting and listening to client objections, delaying acceptance just a little bit longer before I go to trial close or close the sale?

_____

_____

_____

_____

_____

Affirmation

∞

I always know the right time to close with my clients to deliver on my sales goals and in a way that makes my customers ready to purchase.

26

How Are You Being Ultra-high Definition?

~~

We live in an ultra high-definition 4K world. By the time you read this, we may be well beyond that with 8K or better. The cost of high quality visuals is economical, so make sure you have great audio, photos and/or video at all times. This is a cardinal rule for presentations. Regardless of the quality of your media presentation, a mindful presentation explains the step-by-step details of how to actually use your product or service. Everything you present must be demonstrated in the next step, before you attempt a trial close or close. Be mindful and present in the moment and don't over-promise during a presentation. If you do, you risk under-delivering during the next step, the demonstration of your product or service.

Mindful Sales Question for Consideration

Are my presentation tools up to par with what my customers expect? Do they match my product offering and brand standard?

_____

_____

_____

_____

_____

> Affirmation
>
> My presentations improve with every prospect. I present with confidence and deliver great value.

27

Your PRESENT-ation

Your presentation is a present to your potential customer. How you wrap and unpack your product or service, while being present in the moment, will lay the foundation for the rest of the customer experience.

Mindful Sales Question for Consideration

How can I present my product or service in a way that excites my prospects while educating them on the features and benefits?

_____

_____

_____

_____

_____

> ### Affirmation
>
> ∞
>
> I am a present to my clients. I bring joy just like a birthday gift everywhere I go.

28

Stage Time – Present with Mindful Power

~~~~

Presentations today are in person, online via audio only and via full video.

The time is now for you to present your product; and you may believe that you only get one chance. First impressions are critical, and it's important that your product or service be presented in the best light possible. Being mindful during a presentation is to be honest with what your product is, rather than what it is not, or what you want it to be. Be real and if you provide an effective, authentic presentation, your client will ask for a demonstration (trial) of your product or service. Be mindful to answer questions along the way and even use a trial close or two to gauge the interest of your clients.

Mindful Sales Question for Consideration

How do I adapt my presentation and/or demonstration to connect face-to-face? How do I adapt my presentation and or demonstration to connect via video?

_____

_____

_____

_____

_____

Affirmation

∞

I know I provide the right presentation to my prospect at the right time presenting the features and benefits of my product/service with confidence and ease.

29

Take it for a Test Drive

∞

Here we go - it's time to put up or shut up. It's time to put your money where your mouth is. This is the time for your potential customer to actually try your product or service. This is the free sample at the food court. Will your product or service engage the senses of your potential customer in a positive way? Will it evoke a positive or negative emotion? If you over-promised during the presentation phase, you may find your customer is not buying what you are selling. If the "moon and stars align," your client should know what they are getting. There should be few or no surprises. That is the sign that you are on your way to the next step, which is trial close.

Mindful Sales Question for Consideration

How can I increase my ability to connect with prospects in the demonstration and presentation steps in order to be more mindful in the sales process?

_____

_____

_____

_____

_____

> ### Affirmation
>
> I have fun when I demonstrate my product/service to my prospect. I do this in such a way that they are assured to see, feel and know the value my product brings to their world

30

Don't Panic!

~~~

Being mindful and authentic are critical elements during the demonstration phase. Celebrate if everything goes according to plan, as you described during the presentation step. If things do not go well (like your product or service breaks down during the demonstration), do your best not to panic. Breathe in and out. Explain to your potential client what happened, and, more importantly, what you will do to correct the deficiency to give them peace of mind that it will not happen again. If it does, your have a sound, viable plan to make a quick correction.

Mindful Sales Question for Consideration

When I feel uneasy or nervous in the sales process, how can I ask my inner wisdom or my intuition what belief is being triggered and how I can shift that to peace?

_____

_____

_____

_____

_____

> ### Affirmation
>
> ∾
>
> I am at ease in all steps of the presentation and demonstration sales process. I know my product inside and out. I speak to it and about it with confidence.

31

Plan B – Have One in Your Pocket

～

The famous boxer Mike Tyson actually said it best. "Everyone has a plan until they get punched in the mouth." Anticipate positive and negative experiences during the sales process. Allow us to say it again - anticipate things going well, and also things going not well. Also, prepare for the unknown. You may not know every outcome; however, you can prepare yourself for how you respond when things happen.

Mindful Sales Question for Consideration

What is my plan B in the many steps of the Mindful Sales process?

_____

_____

_____

_____

_____

Affirmation

∞

I am flexible when I need to adapt my presentation and demonstration. I do so to meet the needs of my customer.

32

Evolutionary Budgeting

~~~

You may find that budgets change as the sales process evolves. It's amazing to see that money can appear as you build rapport with your potential customer(s). Throughout qualification, additional resources may be identified such as sponsors, or money in the budget that can be added with the proper business justification. Remember, this may be the voice in your head telling you, "there is no way this customer can afford my product or service." Shift your thinking to believe the money can be found and that budgets are often just a placeholder on a financial statement that may be adjusted with ease and joy.

Mindful Sales Question for Consideration

How can I positively adapt the income side of my budget? How can I positively adapt the expense side of my budget? How can we make the budget work?

_____

_____

_____

_____

_____

> Affirmation
>
> ∞
>
> I know the budget of my sales process is flexible in ways that are always for my highest and best.

33

Dance Like Nobody is Watching

∞

Go all in during your demonstration. Geek out - be the person in the middle of the dance floor that everyone is talking about. Just be you and if you are passionate about your product, it will show. The proof is in the pudding, the cream rises to the top. This is your moment. As Lee Ann Womack so eloquently sang, "I hope you dance!"

Mindful Sales Question for Consideration

How can I add a little levity to the sales process when it starts to feel too serious?

_____

_____

_____

_____

_____

> ### Affirmation
>
> ∞
>
> I have fun representing my company to all leads, prospects and clients. My ability to have fun increases my ability to sell.

34

Keep the Demons out of Demonstration

~~~

If you experience a product or service failure during your demonstration, be mindful to pause and acknowledge the deficiency, rather than avoiding the problem. Think of the Wizard of Oz saying "Pay no attention to the man behind the curtain." Honesty is a key part of your business integrity. Call out the error, and more importantly, share how you are going to fix it or ensure it will not happen again.

On a recent visit to Hawaii, we learned a legendary story of mischievous, fictitious trolls called Menehunes which appear and wreak havoc in life. Luckily, you can blame these imaginary characters and laugh at the situation instead of focusing on the negative mindset.

Remember, what you think about you bring about. Negative thoughts such as, "there is no way this customer is going to buy from me," may lead to your actions which prevent the customer from moving forward to closing the sale with you.

Mindful Sales Question for Consideration

How can I make my demonstration more personal and engaging for my customer? How can I create a demonstration experience vs simply a sales demonstration by making my prospect connect more authentically to the product?

_____

_____

_____

_____

_____

Affirmation

∞

I release any fears from my sales process now, assuring greater levels of connection and sales with my leads and, prospects and increasing my repeat business success.

35

The Cream Rises to the Top

～

When in doubt, choose quality throughout the sales process. There is a reason salespeople are sometimes negatively stereotyped. If it feels shady or inauthentic, it probably is. Don't be one of those sales people. If it means slowing down and taking a little more time to "do something right," it's worth it in the end. Your potential customer will see this. Even if they don't buy from you, the quality they experience will resonate and will likely lead to referrals or something better.

Mindful Sales Question for Consideration

Am I willing to be the #1 sales person in my company? How am I making daily steps in that direction? If I am not, why not?

_____

_____

_____

_____

_____

> ### Affirmation
>
> ∞
>
> My sales process is always improving and my close rate is increasing as a result. I am happy with my ability to deliver success.

36

Would it Help Your Customer?

Asking questions during the Mindful Sales process demonstrates respect and professionalism. Ask if a feature of your product or service were to benefit your customer, solve their problems or ease their mind. Simply and respectfully ask questions to confirm their understanding and be open to their response, without judgment, of course.

Mindful Sales Question for Consideration

What are two bold questions I can ask that would invite my customer to connect with me in a more personal way?

_____

_____

_____

_____

_____

> ### Affirmation
>
> ∞
>
> I know the power of a good question in the sales process. I use questions effectively.

37

Quality, Not Quantity

∽

Too much of a good thing can be a bad thing after all. The sales process is a practice, not a "perfect." Read your customer's response to your trial close. Is their response authentic and engaging? Are they leaning in to your question, or are they creating distant space?

Mindful Sales Question for Consideration

What quality of my product am I most excited about? How can I share my personal passion or experience with this product in a way that the prospect gains excitement and is motivated to purchase?

_____

_____

_____

_____

_____

Affirmation

∞

I am quality delivering quality to quality buyers every day.

38

Deals Come in All Shapes and Sizes

∞

Remember that you may need to start small before signing that big deal that sets you up for life. There are countless stories of lottery winners or professional athletes who come into large sums of money, only to find themselves in the same position (or worse) within a short time. Do not be surprised if you attempt to close a sale for a large dollar figure and you are given a small deal instead. Relax, breathe in and out. The customer is doing their due diligence to ensure you can handle a small deal before they bet the farm and make a larger investment in your product or service. Small deals can be very lucrative. They help to pay the bills until the big deal comes in.

Mindful Sales Question for Consideration

What is the most "small" or "medium" deal you have ever closed? Celebrate these as much as you do the "large" deals.

_____

_____

_____

_____

_____

> ### Affirmation
>
> I celebrate every closed sale with joy and gratitude. Each signed deal brings me closer to my goal. There is no big or small in my sales success.

39

Ask for the Business. Always.

∞

Even a bad attempt to close is better than no close at all. Think of Jedi Master Yoda from Star Wars when he says, "Do. Or do not. There is no try."

Mindful Sales Question for Consideration

Who have I not asked for the business? Why? Can you connect to that person today and make the ask?

_____

_____

_____

_____

_____

Affirmation

∞

I am open and willing to ask every prospect for their business.

40

It's a Practice Not a Perfect

~~~

There is an art to the science of selling. There are buying indicators and non-buying indicators that happen throughout the process. Things often go right, but not always. If something goes wrong along the way, forgive yourself. Keep practicing being mindful during sales and your honest, authentic delivery will shine through.

Mindful Sales Question for Consideration

What step in the Mindful Sales process could I be better at? (intention, vision, affirmation, meet & greet, qualification, presentation, demonstration, close/trial close, follow up, gratitude) Spend 15 minutes today practicing that skill. Vision your increased sales success.

_____

_____

_____

_____

_____

Affirmation

∞

I am grateful each day for the opportunity
to get better as a Mindful Sales professional.

41

Expect a Return on Your Engagement

~~~

There is such a focus in the world on Return On Investment (ROI). Perhaps the brochure which advertises this concept is incomplete, or even wrong and the focus should actually be shifted to a return on engagement. Engage with you target audience. Start a conversation - more importantly, start building a relationship with them. You were taught this in Kindergarten, just be authentic and honest without expecting anything in return.

Mindful Sales Question for Consideration

What is expectation? What is expectancy? How can I set an energy around me that I expect only good things to come my way? Watch the good show up in your world!

_____

_____

_____

_____

_____

Affirmation

∞

I know and trust that every call I make and every lead I connect with sends positive energy into the world and is returned to me in mindful, successful ways. I plant seeds each day for the next sales contract.

42

Nothing Comes for Free

The price of a product or service is the opportunity cost of something else. As you enter in to discussions on price, this should feel natural and without judgment. Everyone wants a great deal in the world of commerce. Remember that you do not need to give your product or service away, or discount the product without a valid and reciprocal compensation.

Mindful Sales Question for Consideration

How am I circulating my good energy today? (Note: energy in all forms, money, smiles, wisdom, knowledge etc.) How do I open my receiving channels for more good to come into my life personally and professionally?

_____

_____

_____

_____

_____

Affirmation

∾

I honor the Law of Circulation that requires me to be compensated. While I may not make money on every deal, good works, good money and good experiences are always coming my way. The world is always working for my good.

43

Follow Up

~~~

Early in our careers, we learned that some sales professionals disappear after a contract is signed or the deal is done and the operations team takes over. This is a fatal flaw and a blind spot for many sales non-professionals. Be mindful of keeping the conversation going after the sale. Ask how the customer is enjoying the product and offer assistance if things are not going as well as they could be.

Mindful Sales Question for Consideration

How am I following up with my customer? How am I following up with my internal sales support team? How am I following up/checking in with myself to assure I am being as mindful as possible as a sales professional and kind person?

_____

_____

_____

_____

_____

> Affirmation
>
> ∞
>
> I approach my follow up tasks with gratitude knowing they are fun and fantastic.

44

Follow Up on the Business That Did Not Even Happen

∞

Times change, budgets change. A potential customer in one moment may be promoted in the future, change jobs or come into new resources. You never know until you follow up with them.

Mindful Sales Question for Consideration

Who can I reconnect with today who did not buy from me just to check in with mindful care and concern? How can I be a good human today?

_____

_____

_____

_____

_____

> ### Affirmation
>
> ∞
>
> I demonstrate my professionalism as a Mindful Sales person by following up with leads who did not buy from me to demonstrate my commitment to being of service in each and every moment.

45

Walk Beside Each Customer

Every customer comes to you with a different mindset. A Mindful Sales approach is to not view yourself as better or worse than your customer. You may have the knowledge or insights on your product which they do not have. Share this knowledge with kindness and professionalism. Avoid condescending behavior that puts the customer down or makes them feel inferior. Walk beside each customer as an equal partner throughout the sales process.

Mindful Sales Question for Consideration

How am I demonstrating my empathy for my customer today?

_____

_____

_____

_____

_____

> ### Affirmation
>
> ∞
>
> I meet my clients where they are and walk with them to make sure they get the right product at the right time for the right and perfect price.

46

Sales is Leadership & Leadership is Sales

Choose to demonstrate leadership as a Mindful Sales professional. Have you ever been told, "you're just in sales, you don't understand how our business operates?" (Or similar). Sales professionals who choose to study and enhance their leadership skills will see that results are tied to this trait. Lead and guide your customer with the utmost honesty and integrity.

Mindful Sales Question for Consideration

How am I demonstrating skills of leadership today? (honesty, integrity, communication, decision making, accountability, inspiration, creativity, etc.)

_____

_____

_____

_____

_____

Affirmation

∞

I know my thoughts, beliefs and actions as a Mindful Sales professional lead everyone in my organization to greater levels of personal and professional success.

47

Did I Hear You Say Thank You?

～

As a gracious host and Mindful Sales professional, you should thank your customer verbally and in writing. Be authentic. We heard a story of a respectable company investing $1 million with a county in Florida to show they were serious about their proposal. They did not win the business. One of the county commissioners actually said the words, "Thanks a Million," during a public hearing. We honor venture capital for all of the good it represents. Be sure to honestly and authentically find a way to mindfully thank your customer for their business. If your keep an ethical guide here, you may scale your thank you gift(s) to the size of the business. An authentic, hand-written thank you can be priceless compared to a high-dollar thank you gift. Use your intuition and let your conscience be your guide.

Mindful Sales Question for Consideration

How many "thank you" messages have I sent this week? Take a moment to send a "snail mail" card, call, email, text or other form of communication to someone you are grateful for. Be conscious of ways that gratitude shifts your energy and sales success.

_____

_____

_____

_____

_____

Affirmation

∽

I know the power of my gratitude expands what I have to be grateful for.

48

Gracious Guest? Maybe? Maybe Not?

You can control many things during the Mindful Sales process; however, your customer's gratitude may not be aligned with your expectations. Do not judge.

Mindful Sales Question for Consideration

Even though I did not sell to this prospect, how could I have made that person's day just a little bit better? A smile, a compliment, hug or handshake is sometimes all a person needs to shift from a negative to a positive in their day.

_____

_____

_____

_____

_____

Affirmation

∞

I bless and thank even the most frustrating of leads, prospects and clients knowing that we all can have a bad day once in a while. Blessings cost me nothing and make me a magnet for good.

49

Analysis Paralysis – What Can You Do To Make It Better or Worse?

∞

In the movie *Bridge of Spies*, Tom Hanks' character questions a man on trial for treason, "You don't seem alarmed?" The man responds, "Would it help?"

If you are worried during any part of the sales process, for any reason, does it help? Where do you stop to over-analyze your situation without meaningful action? We invite you to utilize your Mindful Sales techniques. Breathe, center and stay present in the moment. Affirm what you want to have happen.

Mindful Sales Question for Consideration

What could I have done to make this sales conversation even better for me? For the customer? For my sales support team?

_____

_____

_____

_____

_____

Affirmation

I know the power of breathing and centering keeps me grounded and moves my Mindful Sales process forward.

50

Everything is Perfect, All the Time.

※

You will win some sales and you will lose some sales. Things will go right and things will go wrong. You may lose a sale after doing "everything right." You may win a sales after something (or everything) goes wrong. Remember that all is working toward your highest and best, at all times. Celebrate and be grateful for the wins and losses, and forgive yourself.

Mindful Sales Question for Consideration

What am I willing to give for something better in my next sales experience? What did I learn from the perception of the mistake I made in this sales conversation?

_____

_____

_____

_____

_____

Affirmation

∞

I forgive myself for all the mistakes I have made in the sales process and move forward with trust that the next sale is a good sale.

51

Honoring the Objection with Opportunity

Overcoming objections is a part of the sales process. It would be nice if a potential customer agreed with everything you presented and did not have any questions. That is not common or realistic. Anticipate objections and look forward to them. The customer is communicating their concerns, which is an opportunity for you to demonstrate your professionalism in action.

Mindful Sales Question for Consideration

What objection do I keep hearing? How can I prevent that objection from coming up in my next sales conversation?

_____

_____

_____

_____

_____

> Affirmation
>
> ∞
>
> I am thankful for objections as opportunities for me to be a better, more Mindful Sales professional.

52

Begin Again

~~~

Win or lose, the sales cycle never ends. If you successfully converted the sale, you follow up to make sure everything is going well and ask for future business/referrals. The timing of this may vary, depending on the lifecycle of your product or service. If you did not convert the sale, always be mindful, courteous and professional. Remember, you will win future business based on how you act when you lose business.

Mindful Sales Question for Consideration

What can I do in the next five minutes to move my Mindful Sales cycle forward? Keep it simple. One thing.

_____

_____

_____

_____

_____

> **Affirmation**
>
> I know there is no beginning and no end to the Mindful Sales process so I keep going with positive confidence and gratitude.

Bonus Tip

Mindful Sales is Art & Science

You can follow a checklist, do everything "right" and you will still lose business. Embrace the art of using Mindful Sales and know that it takes practice and it is rarely perfect.

Mindful Sales Question for Consideration

How am I creating art with my Mindful Sales process? How am I using science and the data my company provides to increase my sales process?

_____

_____

_____

_____

_____

Affirmation

∞

My intentions for positive sales results makes my world a better place.

Bonus Tip

What You Visualize You Actualize

In those moments when you brain says you can't or won't make the sale, use your power of visualization to trick your brain into seeing the opposite - success. Take a moment to see a positive conclusion to the sales you currently have in your funnel.

Mindful Sales Question for Consideration

What am I visualizing as sales success for me, my family and the world around me?

_____

_____

_____

_____

_____

Affirmation

∞

I visualize my sales success each day. This success makes me feel good.

Bonus Tip

Become What You Believe

∽

Override any place you believe you will not make the sale. Take a moment at your work station, desk, or on the sales floor to remember you believe in you.

Mindful Sales Question for Consideration

What am I becoming as I believe in my ability to sell with mindful practices?

_____

_____

_____

_____

_____

> Affirmation
>
> ∞
>
> I believe in the power of the Mindful Sales process to transform my sales process with ease, fun and joy.

Bonus Tip

Self Care is Not Selfish

All sales professionals reach a tipping point of exhaustion. Listen to your body when it asks for a break. Everything works better when you unplug it, even if just for a minute. Allow yourself to unplug take a 10 minute break, drink a glass of water. Putting yourself first puts you in the best position to sell to others.

Mindful Sales Question for Consideration

How will I take better care of myself mentally, physically, emotionally, spiritually, and financially as a Mindful Sales professional?

_____

_____

_____

_____

_____

Affirmation

∞

I take care of myself during the days, weeks, months and years of the sales process knowing when I take better care of me I can take better care of my customers and family.

Bonus Tip

Team Up With Sales Rock Stars

∽

We added this Mindful tip near the end of the book so you could feel a blanket of support. Sales is not always easy. You may be feeling overwhelmed. Everything is going to be ok.

Mindful Sales Question for Consideration

Who else do I know who could benefit from the Mindful Sales techniques in this book? How can I provide them with this tool so we can support each other more on an ongoing basis?

_____

_____

_____

_____

_____

Affirmation

∞

I am a sales rock star surrounded by sales rock stars. Together we make the world a lighter, brighter place.

Bonus Tip

Just Do It

Where do you need to give yourself permission to just try? If you are in a position where you think you need a little more training, more experience or knowledge, recognize that sometimes we just have to leap and trust that the net will appear. Do something new in your presentation today. No matter what you will learn and refine.

Mindful Sales Question for Consideration

What will I "just do" today to be a more Mindful Sales professional?

_____

_____

_____

_____

_____

Affirmation

∞

I am committed to using my Mindful Sales techniques to help me grow my income and impact in the world.

Bonus Tip

Guilt to Gratitude

~~

It's natural to feel a little guilty for attaining your sales goal or even not hitting the sales goals. Maybe you make more money than a co-worker in bonus, or have a nicer thing than your neighbor. Today release any feelings of guilt and choose to be grateful for the people you have been able to positively impact with your product or service.

Mindful Sales Question for Consideration

How can I show gratitude to myself for what I have learned and implemented from my study of this book?

_____

_____

_____

_____

_____

Affirmation

∞

I am grateful for my choice to be always being a better Mindful Sales professional.

Congratulations on your commitment to your own personal mindfulness practice by reading and applying these 52 tips!

You may notice that we have been careful to not overuse the word "meditation" in this book. Meditation is a powerful tool of mindfulness, but not the only tool.

Now continue your own Mindful Sales journey. At the beginning of this book we invited you to consider what your associations were with the word "sales". No matter your answer at the beginning, we hope this book, with its tips, questions and affirmations has helped you to recognize that the sales process is a truly natural life process. All of us in some way are sales professionals. Why? Because we are all working to influence one another. A car salesperson is opening the sales experience to someone in need of a car. This is also true for the parent inviting a child to change a habit or behavior.

It's time we recognize that we are all human beings, not human doings. We trust that Mindful Sales and the steps in the pathway will help you create a new level of success for you or invite you to refine an already successful sales path.

For more on Mindful Sales visit:
www.MindfulSalesTraining.com

Ask us about:
- Mindful Sales Keynote Talks
- Consulting
- Authorship
- Events
- Coaching

Acknowledgments

∞

"There is a power for good in the Universe and you can use it."
- Ernest Holmes

Writing a book is a work of heart, a commitment to allowing love to fall through your fingertips onto a blank white page. It is the daily practice of not being perfect and holding a mindful vision while it comes each day into clarity. It is the process of cut and paste and cut again. It's leaving things on the cutting room floor and tagging others for future books. We have found this process is an act of love and power to let go and let God. To all that and more, we surrender. Done is better than perfect.

We would like to thank Spirit for bringing us together and continuously inviting us to live, learn, laugh and grow. We give thanks for our "interesting" life path of personal growth and professional opportunities.

We know the power of of our friends and family both biological and chosen, from coast-to-coast and continent to continent. You know who you are and you know we love you.

Thank you to our clients past, present and future. Thank you to the associations, corporations, and all who see the vision of Mindful Sales, and a world that works for everyone.

We want to thank so many people who saw the power of this work and pushed us to use it. At a time like this you know you will forget someone. Please forgive us as we name those on our hearts and minds today who most immediately touched the pages of the book that went from concept to print in 56 days. Yes 56 days.

Thank you to our editor, David Goldberg, designer Andrea Cosantine, website team at Blue Zenith, our mindful poster design team, Lauren Graphic Design, and our Everyday Mindfulness Show podcast support team Rick Pontalion and Jenifer Silence.

There is a power in the Universe that brought all the pieces of Mindful Sales together, so we give thanks to that. And so it is.

With mindfulness and gratitude,

Holly & Eric

Resources

Biofeedback and *Mindfulness In Everyday Life Practical Solutions for Improving Your Health and Performance,* 2019, Inna Khazan, Ph.D.

Everyday Mindfulness From Chaos to Calm In A Crazy World, 2019, Holly Duckworth, CAE, CMP, LSP

Mindful Leadership The A to Z Guide For Stress-Free Leadership, Holly Duckworth, CAE, CMP, LSP

About the Authors

Holly Duckworth, CAE, CMP, LSP is a trailblazing keynote speaker and applied mindful leader. Mindfulness for some is a lesser known word that also creates interesting energy. Some embrace it, others are put off by the word itself. She has personally experienced the outward results of mindfulness as a leadership advisor. As a contributor to the New York Times, Producer/Host of the Everyday Mindfulness Show, and columnist to countless industry publications, she works with stressed-out leaders to create peace, presence and profits. Holly's career began in the world of nonprofits and volunteer leadership teaching thousands of association staff and volunteers how to "reboot" for success. Today she takes the best of her strategic vision expertise and blends it with mindful leadership practices and her event background to curate experiential events that change hearts, minds and companies.

Our world has become mind-less. Through mindfulness training, Holly works with you to know what mindfulness is and what it is not andnapplies mindfulness techniques to produce more productive and profitable organizations.

Holly was named 2019 and 2019 Most Influential Leadership and Strategist by BizBash Magazine, Meetings Today 2018 Trend Setter for her applied mindfulness work and 2016 Smart Meetings Woman of the Year. Holly's current book, *Everyday Mindfulness: From Chaos & Calm In A Crazy World,* is an Amazon Top New Release, *Mindful Leadership: The Stress-Free Guide to Leadership* is a best seller and her award-winning book, *Ctrl+Alt+Believe: Reboot Your Association For Success*, has won two national awards. Holly believes mindfulness builds leaders and organizations that work for everyone.

Eric Szymanski is an award winning American hospitality industry professional with extensive sales and marketing leadership experience. Eric has demonstrated success in leading high-performing sales teams through planning, implementing and monitoring actionable sales and marketing plans at hotels and resorts of all sizes, including city-center, convention district, airport and attractions areas. He has a proven track record of success at all levels through the achievement of both individual and team goals for several first tier, globally recognized brands. Throughout his career, Eric has created authentic, world-class experiences while volunteering at all levels in several meetings industry associations. In 2018, Eric was recognized with the top individual sales award in his convention sales division. In 2002, he was recognized as Caterer of the Year by the Orlando, Florida Chapter of the National Association of Catering Executives. He is an avid runner, choral music performer and father of twins who entered college in the fall of 2019.

To Book Eric for speaking, coaching or consulting, contact: www.LeadershipSolutionsInternational.com

Other Books by Holly Duckworth

Available on
www.LeadershipSolutionsInternational.com
or Amazon.com

Everyday Mindfulness:
From Chaos To Calm In a Crazy World

Mindful Leadership:
The A to Z Guide For Stress Free Leadership

Ctrl+Alt+Believe:
Reboot Your Association For Success

Made in the USA
Las Vegas, NV
17 August 2021